ॐ

KASHMIR SHAIVISM

The 36 Principles

How these Principles coexist,
Why they matter.

Ashwini Kumar Aggarwal

जय गुरुदेव

ISBN13: 978-93-48012-64-7 Paperback Edition
ISBN13: 978-93-48012-87-6 Hardbound Edition
ISBN13: 978-93-48012-43-2 Digital Edition
Full color interior

Title: **Kashmir Shaivism The 36 Principles**
Author: **Ashwini Kumar Aggarwal**

Printed and Published by
Devotees of Sri Sri Ravi Shankar Ashram
34 Sunny Enclave, Devigarh Road,
Patiala 147001, Punjab, Bhārat

https://advaita56.in/ The Art of Living Centre
https://www.artofliving.org/

Devotees Library Cataloging-in-Publication Data
Aggarwal, Ashwini Kumar.
Language: English. Thema: QDTM QRVK2 WZSJ 2A 6CA
BISAC: OCC012000 BODY, MIND & SPIRIT / Mysticism
Keywords: 1. Gross and Subtle Elements. 2. Love Beauty Strength.
Typeset in 12 Segoe UI

22nd November 2025, Guruji visits Zirakpur – gladdens all – infuses vision+will, restores faith in ethical work. Margashirsha Masa, Shukla Paksha Dvitiya Tithi, Jyeshtha upari Mula Nakshatra, Hemant Ritu, Dakshinayana.

Vikram Samvat 2082 Kalayukta, Saka Era 1947 Vishvavasu

1st Edition November 2025

जय गुरुदेव

Dedication

Sri Sri Ravi Shankar

who taught us to honor, revere, respect all

during Maha Shivaratri night 2016 or 2017 at Ashram, Gurudev mentioned the 35th principle Shakti and 36th principle Shiva

Acknowledgements

Lord gives darshan at 9:30pm on 22nd Nov at Sector 33 Chandigarh after a beautiful engrossing Soaking-in-Bliss Satsang and Meditation from 5:45 to 7:45pm at Palms Banquet Zirakpur.

Inspiration from Jagjit Singh ji to throw light on Kashmir Shaivism as we evolve in our journey of life.

Blessing

Guru tattva is the principal, the wisdom.
Guru is a tattva – an element, a quality inside you.
It is not limited to a body or a form.
Life and the Guru are inseparable.

Sri Sri Ravi Shankar
Navratri, Bangalore Ashram 13 Oct 2012

Prayer

oṃ
asato mā sad gamaya ।
tamaso mā jyotir gamaya ।
mṛtyor mā amṛtaṃ gamaya ।

oṃ śāntiḥ śāntiḥ śāntiḥ ॥

Shanti Mantra

O Loving Divine!
Lead us from the shakiness to the firmness.
Lead us from the ignorance to the wisdom.
Lead us from the transient to the eternal.

Peace in our heart, in our body, and in our environs.

Contents

Thee of all friends is true.
Time **Space** Consciousness: **Brahma Vishnu Shiva**
Mind Body Soul: **Love Beauty Strength**
Chemistry Physics Unknown

The mind is transitory. The body and soul are eternal.
The mind perishes. The body and soul remain.
What is other than physics (body), and chemistry (mind) is known as the Soul.

Preface

Kashmir Shaivism = Trika Philosophy = Threefold

Kashmir Shaivism proposes 36 discrete Principles in creation. These are categorized as Trika the Three states of Consciousness.

a) 25 gross aspects of divinity. These make up the visible spectrum of sound and light, name and form.

b) 5+1 = 6 distinct aspects of divinity that have taken a subtle energy body. This form the beginning of the energy-matter phenomena. These can be cognized by intelligent and innocent and clear-hearted men. These occur in deep meditative states to humans, and are also exhibited by flora and fauna and geographical natural phenomena.

The seers state that these six principles serve to obscure what is beyond. These are infamously known as the veils of ignorance.

Actually these six tattva manifest the primal principles of duality, opposites, and all natural and cosmic forces.

And whatever science is unraveling as it evolves, or whatever man grapples with in his quest for spiritual answers, whatever we say gets downloaded from the cosmos to become philosophy, invention, innovation and discovery, nay spirituality.

1. Niyati
2. Kaala
3. Raaga
4. Vidya
5. Kalaa

+1 = 6. Maya

c) 5 distinct aspects of formless divinity. These are the para tattva - the transcendental principles. These are realized by enlightened yogis, and thus cognized in their discourses and teachings. Rare and manifest on earth in certain phenomena, during specific times, and in unique places. We cannot term these 5 principles as matter, and neither as energy. It is technically correct to say these are beyond grasp of man, machine, nature or anything else. These are only divined by enlightened masters, and stated by them, but never in any transactional manner. These 5 aspects cannot be (nay should not be) put in any framework, philosophy, or thought.

Sum = 25 + 5 +1 + 5 = 36 Tattva of Kashmir Shaivism.

i Mahabhuta The Five Gross Elements

The five Maha-Bhuta Gross elements	
01	Prithvi पृथिवी earth
02	Apa आप: water
03	Agni अग्नि fire
04	Vayu वायु air
05	Akasha आकाश ether (space)

ii Tanmatra The Five Subtle Elements

The five Tan-matra Subtle elements	
06	Gandha गन्ध smell
07	Rasa taste
08	Rupa form (sight)
09	Sparsha touch
10	Shabda sound

iii Karmendriya The Five Organs of Action

The five Karma-Indriya Organs of action	
11	Upastha उपस्थ penis (or vagina)
12	Payu पायु anus
13	Pada पाद feet
14	Pani पाणि hands
15	Vaca वाचा speech

iv Gyanendriya The Five Sense Organs

The five Gyana-Indriya Sense organs	
16	Ghrana घ्राण nose
17	Jihva जिह्वा tongue
18	Chakshu चक्षु eyes
19	Tvac त्वच् skin
20	Srotra श्रोत्र ears

v Atmatattva The Five Subtle Fields

The three Antahkarana = Atma-tattva-vyashti Individual field	
21	Manas मनस् mind
22	Buddhi बुद्धि intellect
23	Ahamkara अहङ्कार ego of Iness

The two Atma-tattva-samashti Collective fields	
24	Prakriti प्रकृति nature kinetic
25	Purusha पुरुष awareness potential

vi Avaranatattva The Five Veils

The two Avarana-tattva-sthuLa Gross veils	
26	Niyati नियति place (emotional space)
27	Kaala काल moment (emotional time)

The three Avarana-tattva-sukshama Subtle veils	
28	Raaga राग passion
29	Vidya विद्या knowledge (scientific)
30	Kalaa कला talent

vii Maya The One Covering

The one Maya Covering	
31	Maya माया covering all-enveloping

viii Para The Five Transcendental

What is other than physics (body), and

The three Parāpara enlightened	
32	Shuddavidya ayamatmabrahma soul is brahman
33	Ishvara tattvamasi That am I
34	Sadashiva ahambrahmasmi I am That

The two Para fully enlightened	
35	Shakti शक्ति
36	Shiva शिव

Tattva Hue(spectrum) Emotion(sensation)

1	Earth	Yellow	Humility
2	Water	Deep Cyan	**Joy**
3	Fire	Saffron	Curative
4	Air	Smoky	Evolving
5	Ether (space)	Ivory	**Eternal**
6	Smell	Turquoise	Fragrance
7	Taste	Peach	Delicious
8	Sight (form)	Diamond	**Peace**
9	Touch	Creamy	Pleasure
10	Sound	Transparent	Harmony
11	Penis (or vagina)	Lotus	Enticing
12	Anus	Rose	Exciting
13	Feet	Sunny	Robust
14	Hands	Ebony	Unity
15	Speech	Purple	**Compassion**
16	Nose	Green	**Freedom**
17	Tongue	Pink	Friendly
18	Eyes	Black	Humor
19	Skin	Fair	Soft
20	Ears	Brown	Attentive
21	Mind	Lemon	Mischievous
22	Intellect	Cloudy	Incisive
23	Ego	Deep Red	Pragmatic
24	Prakriti (nature)	Cyan	**Graceful**
25	Purusha (awareness)	Milky	**Witness**
26	Niyati (emotional space)	White	Expansion
27	Kaala (emotional time)	Azure	Spontaneous
28	Raaga (passion)	Red	Attraction
29	Vidya (knowledge)	Light Violet	Intelligence
30	Kalaa (talent)	Silvery	**Enthusiasm**
31	Maya (covering envelope)	Golden	**Beauty**
32	Shuddhavidya (wisdom)	Snowy	Purity
33	Ishvara (That am I)	Blue	**Strength**
34	Sadashiva (I am That)	Indigo	**Truth**
35	Shakti	Vermillion	**Love**
36	Shiva	Sphatik	Auspiciousness

Tattva hexCode(color) DiacriticsUK(pronounce)

1	Earth	#FFFF66	/hjuːˈmɪl.ə.ti/
2	Water	#00B0F0	/dʒɔɪ/
3	Fire	#F4C430	/ˈkjʊə.rə.tɪv/
4	Air	#BFC8C3	Evolving
5	Ether (space)	#FFFFF0	/ɪˈtɜː.nəl/
6	Smell	#40E0D0	/ˈfreɪ.grəns/
7	Taste	#F7BEA7	Delicious
8	Sight (form)	Diamond	Peace
9	Touch	#FEFBEA	Pleasure
10	Sound	Transparent	Harmony
11	Penis (or vagina)	#E4ACB2	Enticing
12	Anus	#FF007F	Exciting
13	Feet	#F7CC3B	Robust
14	Hands	#555D50	Unity
15	Speech	#7030A0	**Compassion**
16	Nose	#92D050	**Freedom**
17	Tongue	#E34B88	Friendly
18	Eyes	#000000	Humor
19	Skin	#FFF4CD	Soft
20	Ears	#BD9A7A	Attentive
21	Mind	#FFFF99	Mischievous
22	Intellect	#AEB2B9	Incisive
23	Ego	#B00606	Pragmatic
24	Prakriti (nature)	#00B0F0	**Graceful**
25	Purusha (awareness)	Milky	**Witness**
26	Niyati (emotional space)	#FFFFFF	Expansion
27	Kaala (emotional time)	#87CEEB	Spontaneous
28	Raaga (passion)	#EE0000	Attraction
29	Vidya (knowledge)	#F6C3FF	Intelligence
30	Kalaa (talent)	#D9DADB	**Enthusiasm**
31	Maya (covering envelope)	#FFD700	**Beauty**
32	Shuddhavidya (wisdom)	Snowy	Purity
33	Ishvara (That am I)	#0000FF	**Strength**
34	Sadashiva (I am That)	#4B0082	**Truth**
35	Shakti	#E34234	**Love**
36	Shiva	Sphatik	Auspiciousness

Pancha Mahabhuta

The five great elements, building blocks of creation.

From Space comes Air.
From Space Air comes Fire.
From Space Air Fire comes Water.
From Space Air Fire Water comes Earth.

It is the five great elements which are the building blocks of creation. Since all of us are directly made up of these, their external presence in our lives plays a major role in our peace, happiness and prosperity. We must try our utmost to have these external elements in abundance, then our internal being gets properly nourished.

Also, our seers and scriptures state methods to keep these tattva in good health, clean and pure. There are various practices that one may adopt in day to day life.

As an example, one can perform Havan. One can perform Puja. One may chant Mantra. One can Sing.

One can keep oneself and one's area tidy. One can adjust eating habits to place and season, and eat healthy and proper.

Exercise like long walks, and Pranayama and Meditation help greatly to balance these tattva and keep them pure within, without.

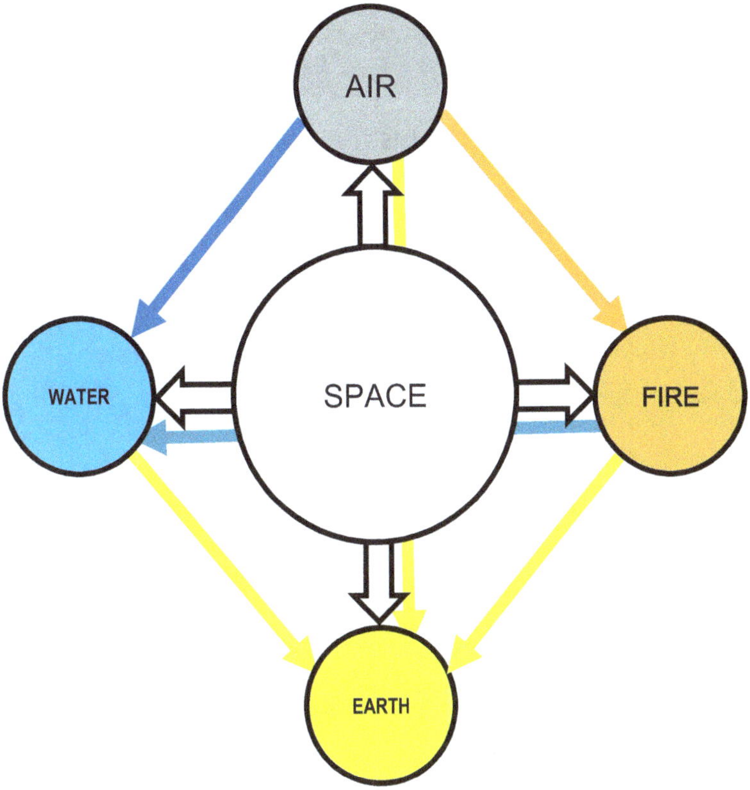
AIR
WATER
SPACE
FIRE
EARTH

1 Earth

Humble is the Earth

Humble is the Earth and that is the starting point. With humility you make a space in the hearts around, with humbleness you find nourishment and grow. A baby is all humility. She is just a bundle of humbleness.

Humility makes you the Emperor, humility endears you to Space and Time, humility is the way forward in Life.

Humility allows you to merge into the Supreme Consciousness. It makes you one with the Divine.

At the Beginning, the 1st element is Humility, also known as Earth. It is a Principle on which the Foundation is laid.

A foundation that can stand the vagaries, that can function in trying circumstances, and that can outlast and be forever.

Humility is Vishnu's hue. Humility is what can maintain. Earth hands over the baton to Water the next spectrum.

Hue: Yellow
Emotion: Humility

Water is Love

Love is water, water is love. We are made of love. We are made of 60% water element. 60% of our body and mind and heart, it is only love.

What is love? What does love mean?

To be able to share yourself. To be able to include the other in yourself. To see his or her or its existence as a part of you. That is love. That is water.

Sparkling Bubbling Huggable Divinity.

Hue: Deep Cyan

Emotion: Joy

Fire is Health

Fire is health. Fire is strength. Fire is that which banishes toxins. That purifies. That cures. That repairs.

Fire makes one feel whole again.

Fire is colored saffron.
Blazing Fiery Rising high.

Fire is your protection, your shield, your defence.
Fire heals, it makes whole, it is highly curative.

Havan Yajna Homa is the standard practice in countless Indian homes to usher sound health for the atmosphere and thereby to the denizens.

A typical Havan takes between 5 minutes to a couple of hours, and it naturally and simply purifies everything – furniture, floor, walls, air, water, earth, and the people and things around.

It banishes the sea of dense & gross & thick emotions and thoughts hanging around, it also cleanses the air and water of virus and bacteria.

Hue: Saffron

Emotion: Curative

Pleasing is the Air

Air ruffling light, touching softly, pleasing entertaining exciting ... just short of fulfilment.

You can't have enough of pleasure, yet you can have as much excitement as you want. The thrill limit simply keeps growing bigger, tantalizing out of reach.

Air keeps one going, moving, yearning.

It makes things function. It makes one creative, productive, elevated. It evolves and is the cause of evolution.

To attain greater joy one may reach out higher, to seek out bigger pleasures one can become more committed, to achieve the absolute one may invest supreme effort.

Hue: Smoky

Emotion: Evolving

Akasha is Citta

Akasha is citta. Space is the sum total. We have heard of cidakasha, not of cidapah, nor cidagni. Space is the primary element. The foundational brick. The basic block. Just as a foundation is the toughest part of men and structures, so is space the densest and heaviest of all elements!

Space is that which cannot be compressed. It is not malleable nor ductile. Space cannot be controlled, modified, subdued or enhanced. It remains as it is.

Space is utmost essential for a fulfilling life, for extraordinary growth and for achieving the supreme. Enough space during childhood becomes the cornerstone for success in the world. A bigger consciousness needs a greater amount of space, or we can say, Consciousness and Space are One. So make sure you keep your personal space private, make sure you have some hours of your own untouched space every single day. Even 20 minutes is enough.

Space is Currency. Space is Gold. Space is the equivalent of Wealth. Not land, not property, not assets. Be very clear. Empty Space. Clear emotional Space. Empty physical Space.The more you have, the richer you shall be, the better you shall function, the easier your path shall be.

Hue: Ivory

Emotion: Eternal

The Sensations

The attributes of the five great elements.

Smell is attributed to Earth. We can smell in presence of earth.
Taste is attributed to Water. We can taste in presence of water
Form is attributed to Fire. We can see in presence of fire.
Touch is attributed to Air. We can touch in presence of air.
Sound is attributed to Space. We can hear in presence of space

These are named Tan-matra. According to His-ability. These frequencies (objects of senses, objects of perception) will have different spectrum bands for each species of life. Also within each species, say a human being, each human's capability to sense will vary. E.g. Some may be able to hear the entire sound spectrum from 20hz to 20khz. However most of us may not be able to hear the lower or higher frequencies. Some may not be able to hear any sound at all. Again in sight, most cannot distinguish all the colors and shades. For birds, animals, insects, plants this sensing spectrum will be much different. This capacity to sense is called Tanmatra. The range of sensitivity. However it is important to note that having a bigger tanmatra in no way impacts one's level of wisdom or state of evolution. In no way is the quality of tanmatra a hurdle on the path of progress. In no way can one's sight or taste etc. deprive us to achieve the highest wealth, power or fame on planet earth. Hence these five tattva are named tan-matra, i.e. those tattva that are not accounted for in the path of spiritual evolution, nor in the path of material success.

Out of all the 36 principles, these 5 principles are not associated with a quantitative or quality factor. (Of course the final five principles, and Maya onwards the six supreme tattva, none of them can be clothed in intellect,reason, philosophy, determinism nor any kind of thought or communication).

So Tanmatra means - to each his own, and that does not impact.

SMELL
EARTH
TASTE
WATER
FORM
FIRE
TOUCH
AIR
SOUND
SPACE

Gandha can touch Divine

Humble is the Earth and its aspect Smell can make us get established in the Divine.

The tattva Earth is Humble. The quality of Earth is called Gandha tattva.

Even though the quantity and quality of earth/humility is graded, its aspect gandha is not. Do you see? Do you understand this? Can you make out the difference? Can tou grasp the essence here?

Never mind. It shall open up bit by bit. Let it be.

Gandha = the ability of smell. The sensitivity of smell. The capacity to experience a range of scents, fragrances. Their variation-quality and their thickness-quantity.

Even though one man might smell a leaky gas line, another boy might not be so sensitive. Even though one woman can enjoy a vetiver or musk scent, some other girl may be unaware of it.

This shall in no way compromise their individual growth trajectories. Nor limit anyone's success.

Hue: Turquoise
Emotion: Fragrance

Rasa can fulfil Divine

Rasa = taste ability. Tanmatra. Specific to an individual, species, or animal. The range and depth of taste one experiences.

Rasa or taste is the key to fulfilment. Most of us feel complete after a good meal. Chefs and restaurants, bakeries and cafes, all are crowded, nay frequented, all over the world.

Even in the forest kingdom, each animal relishes a tasty meal. And so in the deep seas, amphibians and fish, all enjoy a bon appetite. Trees, plants, grass and shrubs, all hunger for fertile soil, enough water and ample sunshine.

Man may not need as much as he eats, however the desire to eat and the fruit of eating makes him feel full.

It is an open secret, delicious food is what lovers crave for. True love strengthens on a fulfilling dinner. Food nourishes the Soul, it is the one element that keeps the Soul alive.

Hue: Peach
Emotion: Delicious

8 Form (Sight)

Rupa can attain Divine

Rupa = form = sight.

How well you see, how clearly you see, the quality of your eyesight. It is a tanmatra, dependent on you. It is dependent on an individual man, species, bird, insect, plant or animal, yet it does not limit anyone to any great extent.

Beauty is a much sought after feature, whether in man, woman, statue or structure. The form that has proportion, that form wins over the rest. The form that has grace, that form takes the cake.

Outer aesthetic value is prized so much that it hypnotizes many. Man loses awareness when a beauty captivates him, man easily surrenders to a beautiful form.

You might ask WHY? The answer is that it brings PEACE. A beauty excites since it evokes peace, a form that has aesthetic value makes one calm immediately.

Hue: **Diamond**
Emotion: **Peace**

Sparśa can hold Divine

Sparśa = touch sensitivity. The aspect of Air tattva.

Sensitivity towards texture, smoothness, softness. The ability to gauge the touch of skin, fabric, chemical or any metal etc.

See nowadays they have metal detectors or chemical detectors, at airports and crossings and hotels.

The ability to sense touch, this 'tanmatra' will in no way impact your ability to achieve victory in life.

Hue: Creamy

Emotion: Pleasure

Śabda can hear Divine

Śabda = Sound. Being able to distinguish faint sounds, being able to hear far off sounds that might carry specific information like an approaching thunderstorm. A train whistle.

The sound of Om. The sounds of nature. The sounds of music. The Sound of Silence.

Even scriptures are called Śabda. The Word of God. Scriptures are ancient texts where pure souls recorded the sounds of nature, humanity, freewill and divinity.

Even the contemporary saints; their words become scripture for later generations. And certainly for their devotees, their word has the power to connect to infinity, to realize Brahman.

In fact, in the case of realized saints, any of their Tanmatra, viz. their fragrance, rasa fervor in their presence, their glance, their touch, any of it can help transcend the samsara. Can part the veil of Maya. Can neutralize one's conditioning, can help one attain Nirvana.

Hue: Transparent
Emotion: Harmony

Have you heard the sound of space? Empty space produces a specific sound. It has a note. Sound tattva is the aspect of Space tattva. Sound is intimately connected to Space.

In school physics we learn that light travels through empty space, but sound needs a medium to travel, it cannot travel in empty space. These guys even identify **photons** of light and phonons of sound. Ha!

I wonder if they really know what they teach???

Only in rarest of the rare places on earth does education really happen. The rest is mere hearsay.

Having said that these five Tanmatra Tattva are individual limits not impacting on individual success, in rare cases having poor vision or taste or hearing may cause danger and harm. However such cases are left unconsidered here. Hence the name Tanmatra.

The Organs of Action

The organs which perform actions.

Penis allows creation and procreation.
Anus does evacuation.
Feet propel us to Move.
Hands enable us to Grasp.

Speech emanates from a combination of *respiration* (lungs provide airflow), *phonation* (vocal cords in larynx vibrate to create sound), and *articulation* (tongue, lips, teeth, soft palate and nasal cavity are the organs shaping the sound).

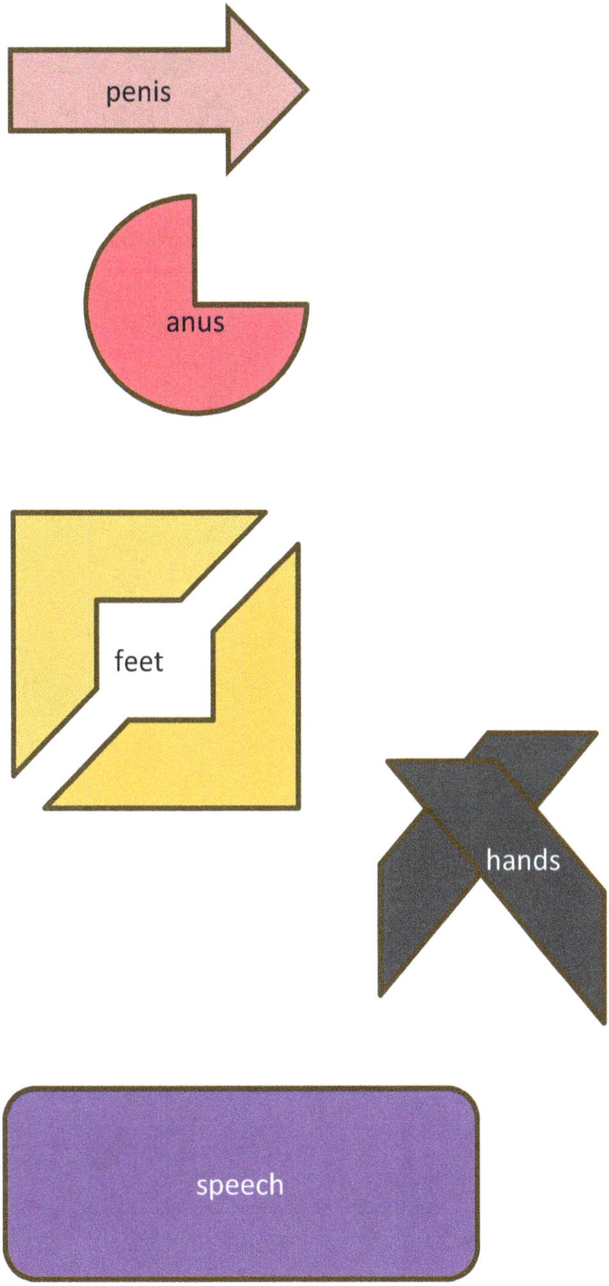
penis
anus
feet
hands
speech

11 Penis

entice `tittilate` arouse *seduce* impel inspire

Penis (or Vagina) the organ of creation, nay procreation. It is known as ***Upastha*** = Stationed in Sheltered location. Situated under the lap.

It keeps our species alive and going forward into the future.

It makes one yearn, dream, hope, and be forever young.

The corresponding Ādhibhūta is called ānandayitavya (i.e. that which is enjoyed, that which secretes).

Hue: Lotus

Emotion: Enticing

12 Anus

excite attract delight stir

Hue: Rose

Emotion: Exciting

13 Feet

robust sturdy rugged solid

Hue: Sunny

Emotion: Robust

14 Hands

unity synergy teamup *cooperate*

Hue: Ebony

Emotion: Unity

15 Speech

compassion kindness caring *empathy*

Hue: Purple

Emotion: Compassion

The Sense Organs

The sense organs by which we experience the sensations.

Smell is sensed by Nose. *Our breath gives us fragrance of earth*
Taste is sensed by Tongue. *Our tongue gives us taste of water*
Form is sensed by Eyes. *Our eyes give us forms by light*
Touch is sensed by Skin. *Our skin gives us touch of air rustling*
Sound is sensed by Ears. *Our ears give us sounds of space*

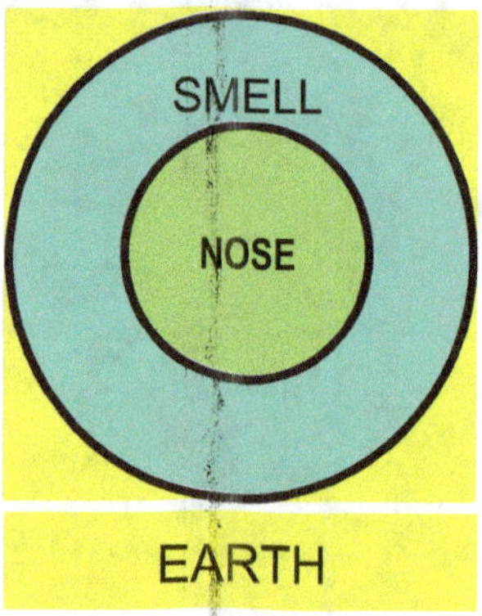

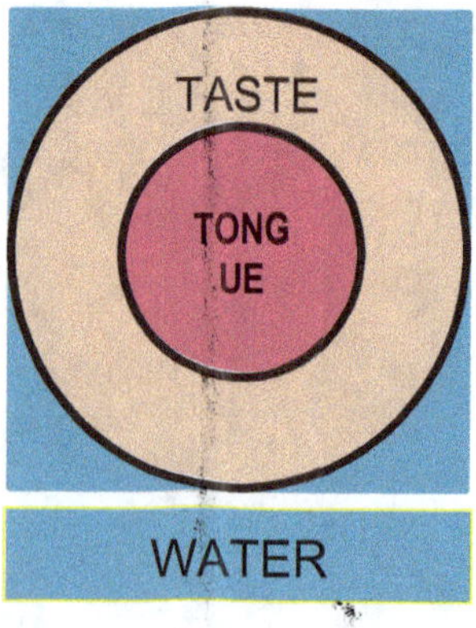

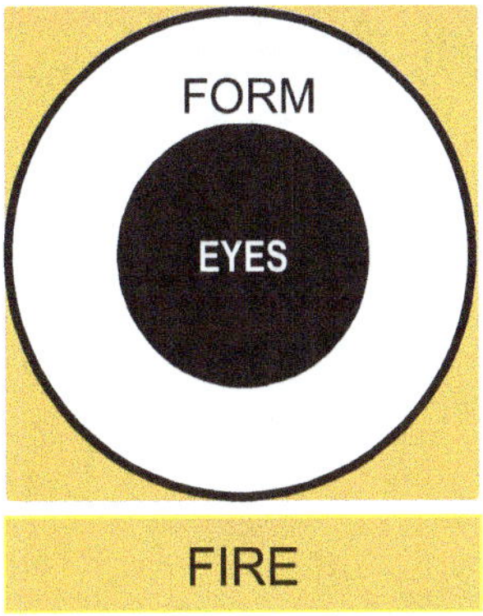
FORM
EYES
FIRE

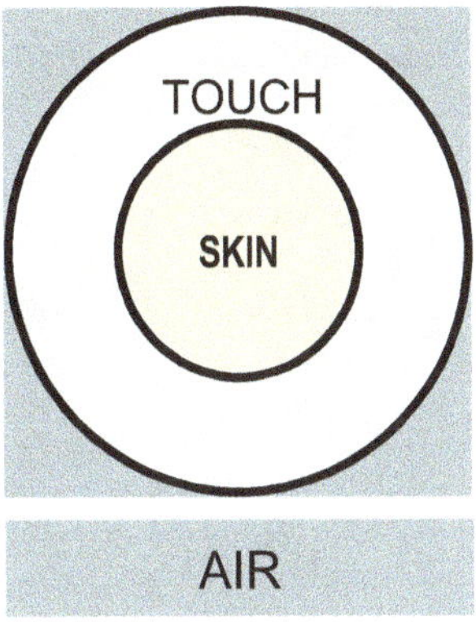
TOUCH
SKIN
AIR

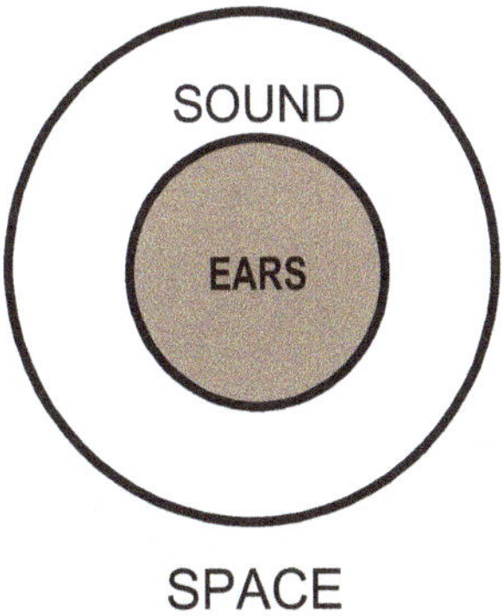
SOUND
EARS
SPACE

16 Nose

freedom `liberty` freewill *relax*

Hue: Green

Emotion: Freedom

17 Tongue

friendly a f f a b l e genial amiable

Hue: Pink

Emotion: Friendly

18 Eyes

humor `sparkling` clear *c*o*n*j*o*in

Hue: Black
Emotion: Humor

19 Skin

soft soothing fair touchable

Hue: Fair

Emotion: Soft

20 Ears

attentive alert mindful *perceptive*

Hue: Light Brown
Emotion: Attentive

The Individual Consciousness

The individual consciousness is known as the Jiva. It is bound to the body of each human being. It reflects the Supreme Reality in its three components, viz:

Mind the controller of Senses and Thought generator.
Intellect the governor of decisive Action by inputs from
the Sensuous-Mind Memory Ego.
Ego the I-ness that enables pragmatic independent life.

(even though Memory has not been mentioned explicitly in the 36 Principles, we show it here for clarity).

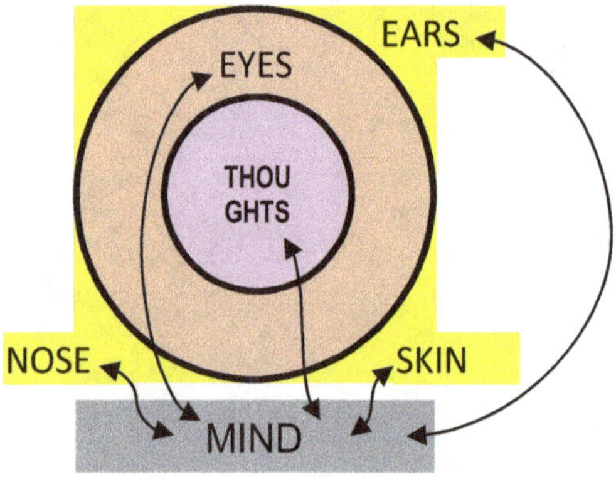

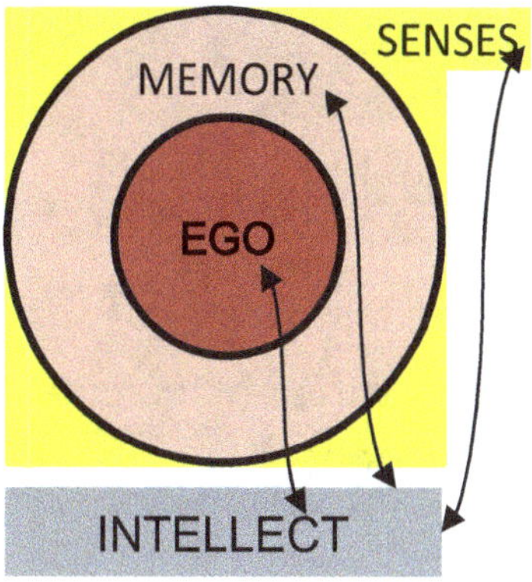
SENSES
MEMORY
EGO
INTELLECT

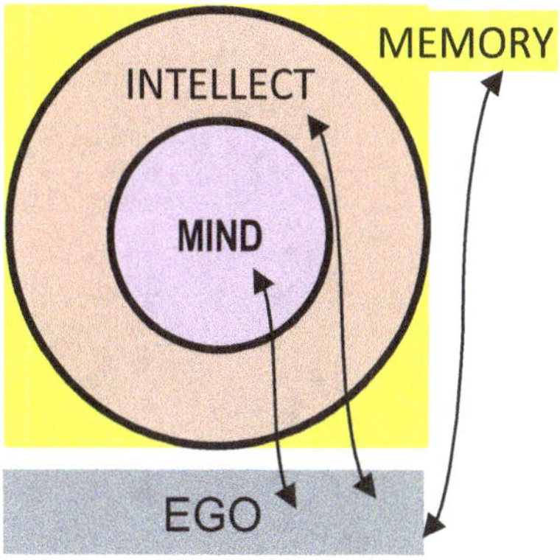
MEMORY
INTELLECT
MIND
EGO

21 Mind

mischief playful prank naughty

O! What can be said about the mind???
It is the KING. All beings follow their mind, the combination of senses and thoughts.

Hue: Lemon
Emotion: Mischievous

22 Intellect

incisive sharp keen astute

O! What can be said about the intellect???
It is the MINISTER. Rarely do beings follow intellect.

Hue: Cloudy

Emotion: Incisive

23 Ego (of I-ness)

pragmatic **sensible** down-to-earth rational

O! What can be said about the ego???
It is FOREVER. Life remains until *ego* is there.

Hue: Deep Red
Emotion: Pragmatic

The Collective Consciousness

The collective consciousness of all beings taken together, whether man, machine, flora, fauna, viz. the summum bonum is known as the Purusha Prakriti.

Purusha is the silent Witness, pure awareness of ALL.
It can be said to be the collective Potential.
Prakriti is the Functional aspect of ALL Nature.
It can be said to be the collective Kinetic.

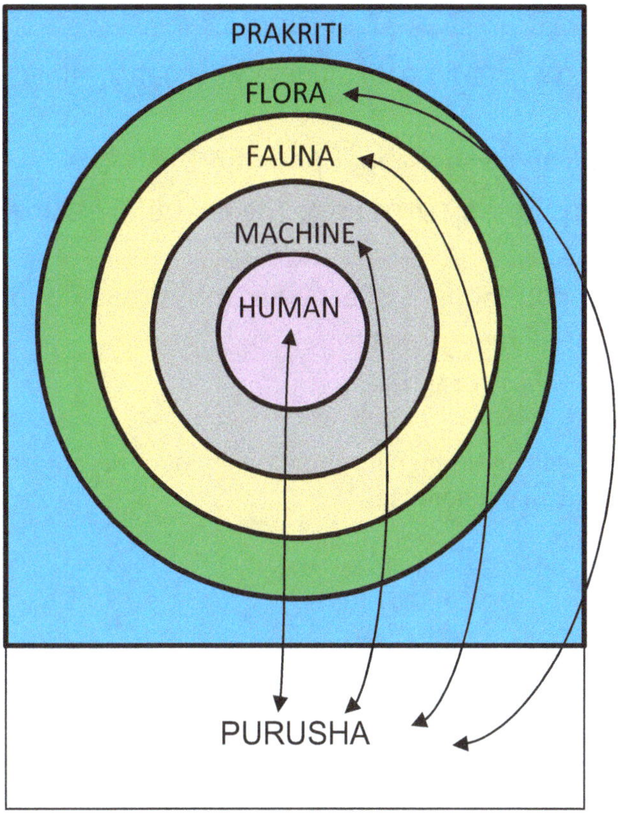
PRAKRITI
FLORA
FAUNA
MACHINE
HUMAN
PURUSHA

24 Prakriti Nature (kinetic)

graceful **dignified** cultivated *elegant* refined

O! What can be said about prakriti???
It is **simply stunning**. The Beautiful Nourisher.

The summum bonum of activities (physical emotional)
of all beings put together
is prakriti.

(here *being* includes man machine rivers mountains flora fauna…and all phenomena).

Hue: Cyan

Emotion: Graceful

25 Purusha Awareness (potential)

witness unshakeable immovable steadfast

O! What can be said about the purusha???
It is safe personified. The calm *observer*.

The summum bonum of buddhis
of all beings put together
is purusha.

Hue: Milky
Emotion: Witness

The Avarana

The yearning and dreams and aims to achieve the best and greatest are known as Avarana. These dreams have individual limits on five levels that can keep on changing, expanding, evolving.

Niyati is the effect of place on one's Intent. Place Aura Space, the ambience has a large say on our Will, our Performance, our Output. Niyati

Kaala is the effect of time on one's Intent. Lack of time or an Abundance of time, both can effect our Will, our Performance, our Output to a large extent. When man makes a determined, committed, sincere effort, then things happen naturally, spontaneously. Kāla

Raaga is an individual's passion or driving force. Enough passion is needed to achieve any aim to satisfaction. Rāga

Vidya reflects an individual's knowledge born of education, perception and attitude. Proper knowledge is essential to achieve the noble and worthwhile. Vidyā

Kalaa is an individual's inherent talent or basic skillset. A very high degree of talent when coordinated with proper attitude, temperament, personality and character delivers the desired bounty. Kalā

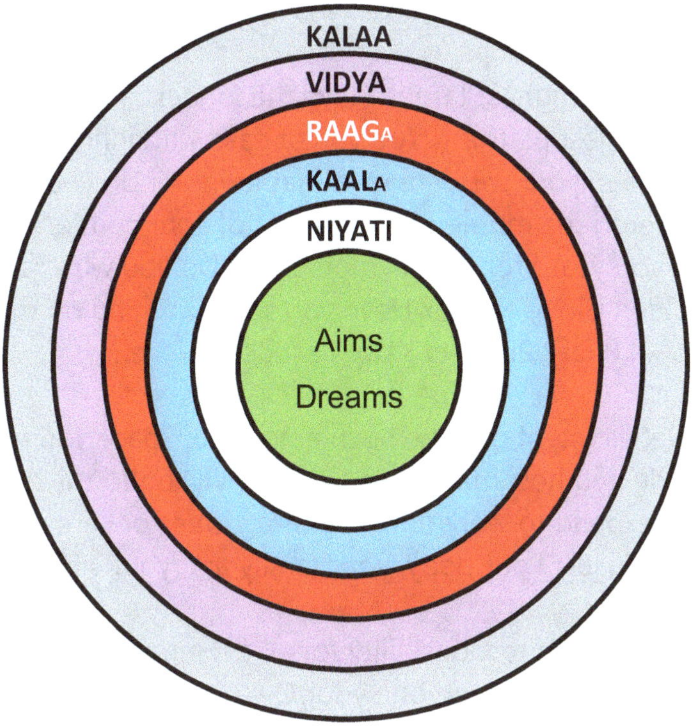
KALAA
VIDYA
RAAGA
KAALA
NIYATI
Aims
Dreams

26 Niyati (Place = emotional space)

What target do you make, what aims do you have?

Make the highest target. Have the longest aim. Go for the biggest platform. Are you at ease with infinity? Can you keep your wits in a royal gathering or do you get flustered the moment you are out of your comfort zone? Do you yearn for the Olympic gold? Do you wish for the Golden Globe award? Have you set your mind on the Nobel Prize? Phi Beta Kappa academic level?

Niyati is Intent of how much emotional Space you have inside and how many Miles you are willing to travel. Can you expand to work for the entire globe...or...are you stuck in just your body, your family and your village?

Can you take responsibility for all of Humanity? Can you make each and everyone your Own? Can you deliver for all of Society? Have you factored in Nature and Flora and Fauna?

Is your Intent BIG enough? Can your Will resound till the ends of time and space?

Niyati = place or space of work, action, phenomena. Infinite beings, yet all have unlimited space. To grow, to move, to happen, the xyz coordinates keep expanding, so all get accommodated nicely.

Niyati is the Limit you set yourself. It is your farthest Boundary. Niyati hands over the baton to Kaala.

Hue: White

Emotion: Expansion

27 Kaala (Moment = emotional time)

Brave is the moment, and brave is the man who seizes the moment, and brave is he who dives spontaneously.

Are you spontaneous? Are you willing unhesitatingly? Are you brave? Do you have the heart?

For the spontaneous, for the courageous, for the brave, time is only a moment. It is only a flash. It is all done in an instant.

Physical time never is, Emotional time is it.

We make watches and wear watches and tie ourselves to impossible goals. We keep watching the time, not knowing that possibility begins outside of time.

Kaala = the specific amount of time for achieving, or acquiring any objective. Even when speeds increase, they never ever come close to actually doing the summum bonum any quicker. The overall goal still remains far far away. Too much time it takes, nay an infinite amount of time is needed to touch the reality, to actualize what one really wants...

When time is dropped the impossible becomes possible. Life is probable outside the limits of time. Kaala hands over the baton to Raaga. The next spectrum.

Hue: Azure

Emotion: Spontaneous

28 Raaga Passion

Passion Dispassion Compassion. Seemingly apart. Yet with a common factor. The realized realizes they are One.

What motivates life? What inspires work? What makes one extend one's hand first? **Attraction**.

Passion to excel. To perform. To achieve. To win.

Raaga = absolute liking for something. The juices that flow when one falls in love. When one gets attracted. When one begins to desire. When no desire is big enough. When all desires get attained, there is still some more to yearn for.

Have the deepest passion to change yourself to the hue of Krishna. Get totally attracted to Krishna. Seek Him.

Yearn for Him with all your Heart.

And you will begin to live. You will laugh. You shall make it. Any and every aim shall fall lightly at your feet.

Hue: Red

Emotion: Attraction

29 Vidya Knowledge (scientific or scholarly)

And how may you tread the path of passion?

What is the means to achieve anything?

Right knowledge. Right education. Right perspective. Right attitude.

Allow a proper education to sharpen your intellect. Allow a good grooming to enhance your intelligence. Allow the best public schooling to make you well-grounded, fully-developed, with a strong character and a cultured personality.

It is the Limit you are willing to traverse. It is the boundary you are willing to Extend.

Vidya = highest state of knowledge. This limit keeps getting wider and wider as man evolves.

Again and again sit at the lotus feet of the Master. Again and again seek the company of the Wise. Again and again have the fusion of Satsang in your life.

Seek out the best schools there are. Get admitted to the schools that excel. And your world shall become rosy and complete. You shall sparkle and glow and radiate.

Hue: Light Violet
Emotion: Intelligence

30 Kalaa Talent

Enthusiasm is the cornerstone of Life. Sri Sri Ravi Shankar Guruji says, "Life is Joy - Life is Love - Life is Enthusiasm".

A talent blossoms with enthusiasm.

Geniuses may be many, but he who is filled with enthusiasm survives and invents, discovers, innovates and expresses fully.

An entrepreneur exhibits talent, enthusiasm, and bravery. To achieve the biggest, to reach the highest, to traverse the longest, your innate skill comes to the fore. It matters how talented you are.

Kalaa = farthest possibilities and probabilities, or any mix of what event can occur in the "infinite"= unfathomed time-space continuum. The number of possibilities just keeps getting bigger. There ain't any last set.

Lord Krishna has been attributed with the highest skillset. The Number 16. All talented and fully skilled. To handle anything, To achieve everything.

Talent is the pinnacle of niyati expanded emotional space, kaaLa spontaneity in action, raaga deep passion, and vidya superior knowledge. Over lifetimes, talent develops bit by bit.

Hue: Silvery
Emotion: Enthusiasm

The Cloud

Maya = that which the senses grasp, that which the intellect governs, and that which the memory stores. This is more or less prone to error, it is purely subjective, it is not the absolute reality. This limit keeps growing as we evolve, or we can say it has no limit.

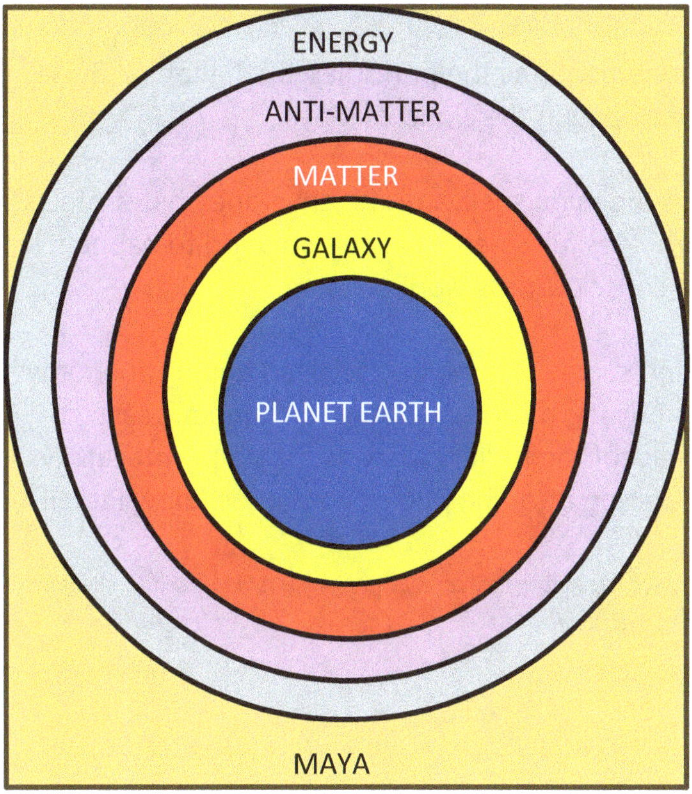
ENERGY
ANTI-MATTER
MATTER
GALAXY
PLANET EARTH
MAYA

31 Maya (covering all enveloping)

A golden veil covers. A beautiful skin hides it all.

All the elements, all the principles, all the tattva, these are enveloped in the cloud of Maya.

Maya is a benign shell, a divine envelope, that protects and provides full safety. It allows creation to happen. It makes consciousness work.

Anything sacred, anything special, anything superior will have a privacy, a secrecy, a limited trumpet. Least broadcast of the triumph achieves it simply gracefully. Then later on it can be published and be known to all.

An unknown laboratory makes history since it had been working in protected seclusion.

Hue: Golden
Emotion: Beauty

The Para

Kashmir Shaivism now hints at principles only the enlightened have realized.

These 5 principles are faint emotions murmurs in the purest stable lionheart.

Anything we say or write about these is purely personal opinion. It may not be close to the Reality. It may be far from the Truth.

5 distinct aspects of The Formless The Unspoken divinity. These are the para tattva - the transcendental principles. These are realized by enlightened yogis, and thus cognized in their discourses and teachings. Rare and manifest on earth in certain phenomena, during specific times, and in unique places.

We cannot term these 5 principles as matter, and neither as energy. It is technically correct to say these are beyond grasp of man, machine, nature or anything else.

These are only divined by enlightened masters, and stated by them, but never in any transactional manner. These 5 aspects cannot be (nay should not be) put in any framework or thought or word!

32 Shuddavidya (wisdom)

White as the white Lotus. White as the spotless Snow.

Pure as the crystal clear waters of the lake.
Pure as the unblemished Soul.
Pure as the fair maiden.

Pure as homemade butter.
Pure as the whitest of white clothing.
Pure as a heart full of love.

Pure as the strong pull of devotion.
Pure as longing.
Pure as tears of gratefulness.

Pure as the silvery fullmoon.
Pure as the soft rays of moonlight.
Pure as a calm tranquil mind.

Hue: Snow white
Emotion: Purity

33 Ishvar (That am I)

Hue: Blue
Emotion: Strength

34 Sadashiva (I am That)

Hue: Indigo

Emotion: Truth

35 Shakti

Hue: Vermillion

Emotion: Love

36 Shiva

Hue: Sphatik Crystal
Emotion: Auspiciousness

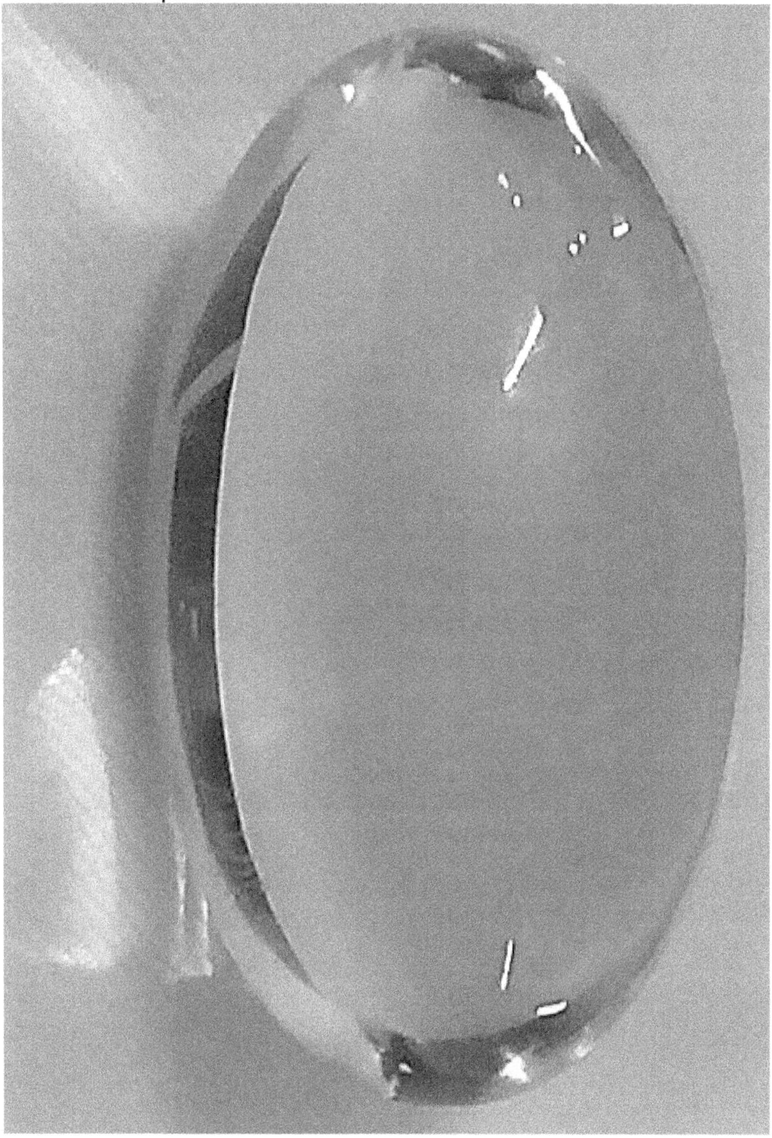

There is a one-to-one relation.

Time = Brahma = Mind = Chemistry.
Space = Vishnu = Body = Physics.
Consciousness = Shiva = Soul = the Unknown.

You can do the practices. You can follow the Master. You can have discipline and good conduct. But being centered is difficult. Very very difficult.

One day you shall have to transcend Time.
Get out of the domain of Brahma.
Get out of the cycle of life and death.
Out of the patterns.
Out of the repetitions.
Out of notions,
assumptions,
concepts,
conclusions.

Then someday the Space shall be left behind.
Get out of the domain of the Preserver.
Get out of the desire to be.

Time is what Creates. Space is what Sustains.
The Mind is Time. The Body is Space.

I am just a traveler. A stranger. Someone from another realm. From far far away.

The **laws**, the **logic**, the **storms** or **passions** मोहः।

but that is just a limited idea. तत्त्व ।

Abundant and Complete it all is. पूर्णमिदं ।

Forever it was, forever it shall be. अनादिः ।

Even if you wish to play, for how long can you play? The same goes for rest and relaxation, soon you shall be up and about, and sooner you shall halt and rest.

asango ham. asango ham. असङ्गोऽहमसङ्गोऽहमसङ्गोऽहं पुनः पुनः ।
Brahmajnanavali Mala of Adi Shankaracharya. Verse 2.

But again there are other possibilities, unexplored realms, ideas and instances that have **seldom** been spoken of, written down, or talked about.

Yoga Vasistha: On Creation: III.15

There is a probability that tends to infinity in so many cases. What exactly is infinity? What is infinite, what does that do?

Is it also governed
by Time? No no.
by Space? Surely not.
Consciousness? Cannot be. Can be?

Take time Out to Do your Practices

Regularly **sit** with Yourself. **Your** personal space is Beautiful. You shall be able to discriminate between the destructible and **in**destructible. This fine dividing thread starts **glowing**.

Do your Practices. Do your daily Sadhana.

Going in a full **circle** you reach the beginning.
Going on a straight **line** you reach ...

is the beginning important?
Certainly there ain't no end?

But logic dictates there has to be a beginning?

Anyways, these are just small games to excite the vibration, the spanda.

For sure i shall breakthrough it all. And be gone.

I wish to go where Thought doesn't exist, where Sound and Sight have no role to play.

Read some Ancient texts

IGNITE YOUR MIND. OPEN YOUR HEART

Time = Thought
Space = Sound
Consciousness = Sight the witness

Time = Love
Space = Beauty
Consciousness = Strength

These Equations are Constructs, the Pillars of Creation. These words by themselves have no meaning. Whatever your heart infuses nay interprets, assumes significance. It may be relative. Then again it may be absolute.

Zero on its own is HUGE. Very very BIG.
Zero is the flame. Inherent brightness. Luminescence.
When it attaches to anything, it gets limited by sight and sound, by time and space, by life and death.

That needs to be dropped. तादात्म्यम् ।

The skin covering zero, त्वक् ।

Veil over infinity needs to be worn thin. शुद्धि-करणम् ।

Then the magic happens. भगवत् प्रकटनम् ।
Nay, the probability for magic arises. ईश्वर-दर्शनम् ।

Sit at the feet of the Master

Once in a while **sit** at the lotus feet of the Master.

परोक्ष-अनुभूतिः
Then the other shore is touched, felt, experienced.

Then one gets absorbed in God. संयम । लयनम् ।

In Shiva. समाधिः ।

And one gets infinite freedom. मोक्षः ।

Infinite strength. शिवः ।
Give yourself prime time. Sacredness. **Reverence**.
Group Practice is always better.

Some, the rarest of the rare, धीराः ।
the very few handful; drop this also. मोक्ष-यिष्यामि ।
They go where nothing can go, nothing has gone.
That is achievable. तत्त्वमसि ।

I shall do it. अहं ब्रह्मास्मि ।

Sanskrit Terms with IAST Transliteration

1	Earth	pṛthvī	पृथ्वी
2	Water	āpaḥ	आपः
3	Fire	agni	अग्नि
4	Air	vāyu	वायु
5	Ether (space)	ākāśa	आकाश
6	Smell	gandha	गन्ध
7	Taste	rasa	रस
8	Sight (form)	rūpa	रूप
9	Touch	sparśa	स्पर्श
10	Sound	śabda	शब्द
11	Penis (or vagina)	upastha	उपस्थ
12	Anus	pāyu	पायु
13	Foot	pāda	पाद
14	Hand	pāṇi	पाणि
15	Speech	vāk	वाक्
16	Nose	ghrāṇa	घ्राण
17	Tongue	jihvā	जिह्वा
18	Eye	cakṣu	चक्षु
19	Skin	tvak	त्वक्
20	Ear	śrotra	श्रोत्र
21	Mind	manas	मनस्
22	Intellect	buddhi	बुद्धि
23	Ego	ahaṅkāra	अहङ्कार
24	Prakriti (nature)	prakṛti	प्रकृति
25	Purusha (awareness)	puruṣa	पुरुष
26	Niyati (emotional space)	niyati	नियति
27	Kaala (emotional time)	kāla	काल
28	Raaga (passion)	rāga	राग
29	Vidya (knowledge)	vidyā	विद्या
30	Kalaa (talent)	kalā	कला
31	Maya (covering envelope)	māyā	माया
32	Shuddhavidya (wisdom)	śuddhavidyā	शुद्धविद्या
33	Ishvara (That am I)	īśvara	ईश्वर
34	Sadashiva (I am That)	sadāśiva	सदाशिव
35	Shakti	śakti	शक्ति
36	Shiva	śiva	शिव

References

Swami Lakshman Joo - Kashmir Shaivism The Secret Supreme-4th 2015-Lakshmanjoo Academy, Oregon USA.

https://www.google.com/search?q=36+elements+of+kashmir+shaivism&oq=36+ele&gs_lcrp=E

Epilogue

At times Stop. Don't always Run.
Ponder hard on your Aim. Dance Clap. Sculpt Sing. Paint.

सर्वे भवन्तु सुखिनः । सर्वे सन्तु निरामयाः ।
सर्वे भद्राणि पश्यन्तु । मा कश्चिद् दुःख भाग् भवेत् ॥
ॐ शान्तिः शान्तिः शान्तिः ॥

When faith has blossomed in life,
Every step is led by the Divine.

Sri Sri Ravi Shankar

Om Namah Shivaya

जय गुरुदेव

Imagine. Think. Dream. Innovate. Experiment. WorkHard.

www.ingramcontent.com/pod-product-compliance
Lightning Source LLC
Chambersburg PA
CBHW062142160726
48282CB00027B/910
* 9 7 8 9 3 4 8 0 1 2 6 4 7 *